I0484627

Contents

About the author

My name is David and I go by Dave. I am 27 years old have a fair amount of irrelevant knowledge about somewhat obscure things. I graduated from the University of Maryland, Baltimore County (UMBC) in 2009 with a BA in Psychology. I have a strong passion for helping people, and Microsoft Excel happens to be a way that I can help many people. I started this adventure in March of 2014, and it has proven to be very rewarding.

You have probably heard the old cliché, "Give a man a fish and he eats for a day, but teach a man to fish and he eats for life". We of course would have to assume that the man could fish far more effectively than I can. Regardless, I believe in the concept that people are best taught to teach themselves. I liken this concept to, "Train the trainer" but I hold nothing but respect for those teaching themselves for personal growth.

I intend to accompany you on your journey, which starts here. I hope that this printed reference guide proves to be helpful and becomes a part of your active desktop collection.

This is your first step. This is a big step. Congratulations, and get ready to unlock your potential with the help of Microsoft Excel!

Logical Functions

And

Why is this function useful?

The And function will analyze multiple logical tests. Each argument must be a full logical test. The And function will only return "TRUE" or "FALSE" depending on the arguments. The key to the And function is that every argument must be true in order to return the "TRUE" value.

This function is particularly nice to pair with other functions like the If function. Nesting an And function inside of an If function will allow you to analyze based on several criteria in the one argument. The If function takes the output of the And function in the first argument.

A few notable details about the And function is how it handles different input. Take a look at the table below to see how certain input is handled.

Description	Formula	Result
True statement	=AND(1+1=2)	TRUE
False statement	=AND(1+1=3)	FALSE
Boolean input	=AND(TRUE)	TRUE
Boolean input	=AND(FALSE)	FALSE
Evaluation of a blank cell	=AND(E6="")	TRUE
Evaluation of a blank cell	=AND(E7=1)	FALSE
Numeric input (1)	=AND(1)	TRUE
Numeric input (0)	=AND(0)	FALSE
Numeric input (anything other than zero. Including negative numbers)	=AND(143)	TRUE
Alpha input	=AND(a)	#NAME?
Multiple true statements	=AND(1+1=2,TRUE,E6="")	TRUE

Description	Formula	Result
True and false statements	=AND(1+1=3,1+1=2)	FALSE

How difficult is this function to use?

This function is very easy to use.

How do I use this function?

1. Open Microsoft Excel and locate the data that you wish to use.

2. Activate the cell where you want to display the result of your logical test.

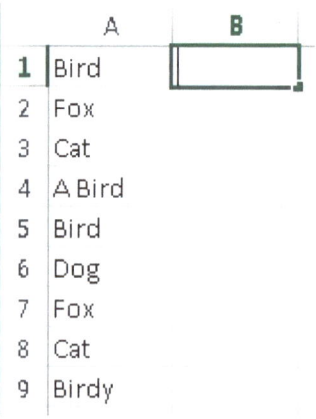

3. Type the And function, "=AND(".

4. Input your first argument, in this example, "A1="Bird"". This argument is the portion that you define the logical test(s) mentioned in the description.

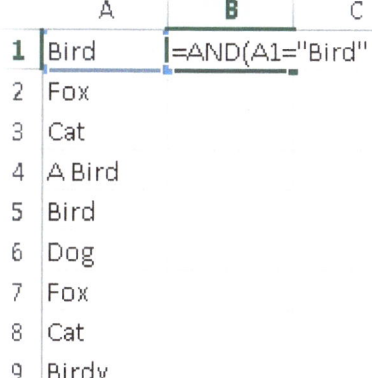

5. Type a comma to move to the next argument.

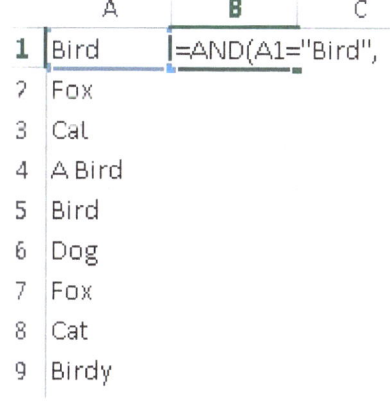

6. Input your next argument, in this example, "A2="Fox"". You can repeat steps five and six to accommodate your needs.

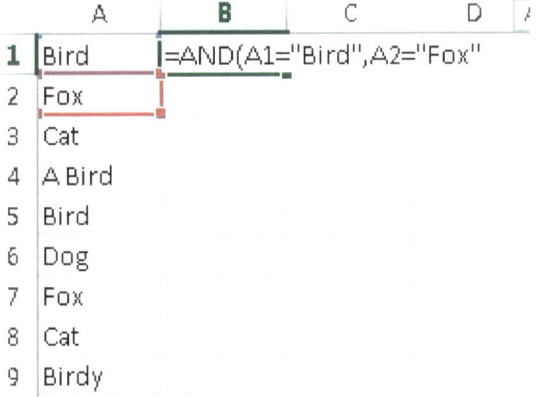

7. Complete the function with a closing parenthesis ")".

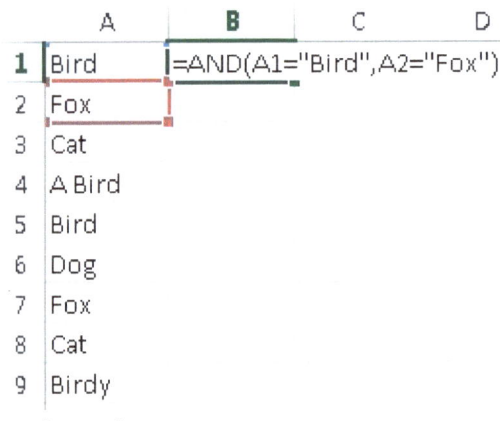

8. Hit "Enter".

9. Congratulations! You have used the And function! Below is an example of what happens when you copy that formula down column B using the Fill Handle.

	A	B
1	Bird	TRUE
2	Fox	FALSE
3	Cat	FALSE
4	A Bird	FALSE
5	Bird	FALSE
6	Dog	FALSE
7	Fox	FALSE
8	Cat	FALSE
9	Birdy	FALSE

False

Why is this function useful?

The False function in Microsoft Excel is particularly useful as a constant. The function itself has some fantastic properties. For one thing, the name is the purpose of the function. Secondly, and somewhat more useful to note, the False function will also work without adding parentheses. The False function already has no arguments so if you are using it within another function then simply typing "FALSE" will give you the same false constant that the False function will give you. The numeric representation of the False function is the value of zero (0).

How difficult is this function to use?

This function is very easy to use.

How do I use this function?

1. Open Microsoft Excel and locate the data that you wish to use.

2. Activate the cell where you want to display the result of your logical test.

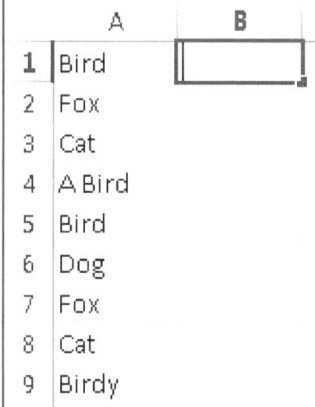

3. Type the False function, "=FALSE()".

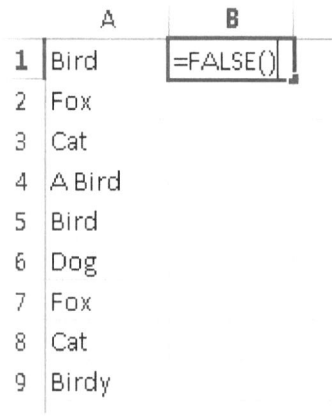

4. Hit "Enter". There are no arguments in this function because it is actually a constant. You can even leave off the parentheses to complete this function.

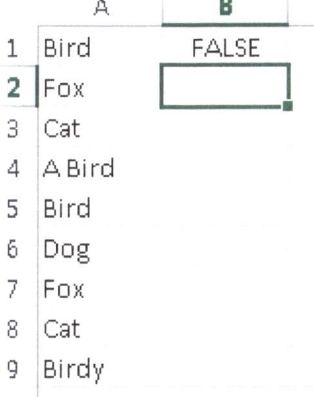

5. Congratulations, you have now successfully used the False function! Remember that you can use this inside any other function that takes a logical argument. The False function will return a constant False Boolean value.

If

Why is this function useful?

The If function will analyze a logical test that you define and give a certain result based on the outcome. You are also able to define exactly what happens if the logical test is true or if the logical test is false.

How difficult is this function to use?

This function is moderately easy to use but it can get complex if you take advantage of your ability to nest functions in the true and false conditions.

How do I use this function?

1. Open Microsoft Excel and locate the data that you wish to use.

9

2. Activate the cell where you want to display the result of your logical test.

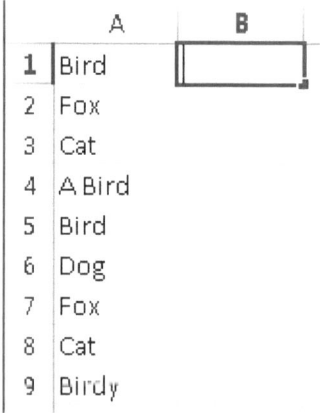

3. Type the If function, "=IF(".

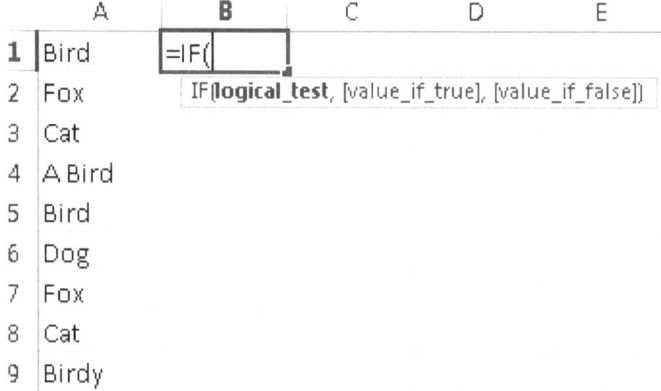

4. Input your first argument, in this example, "A1="Bird"". This argument is the portion that you define the logical test mentioned

in the description. This can hold as many types of logical tests as you can think to throw at it. This example is pretty simple and straightforward but I include more examples of logical tests below.

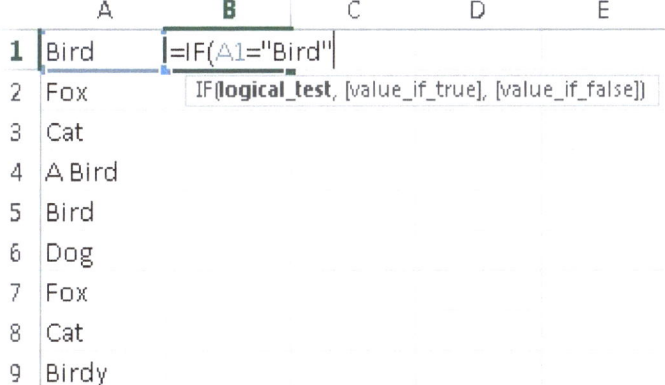

5. Type a comma to move to your next argument.

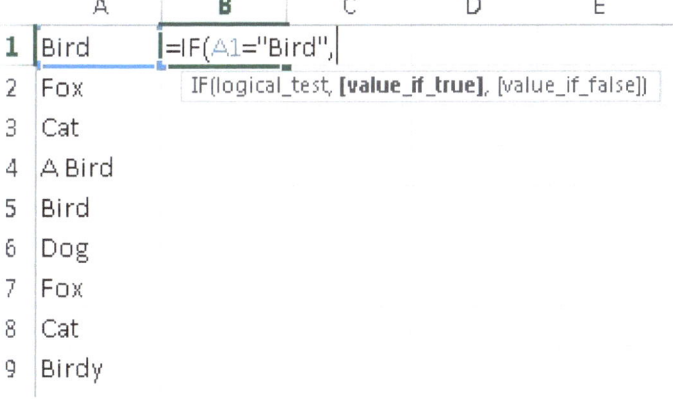

6. Input your second argument, in this example, "It's a Bird". This argument is what is displayed if your logical test (from step 4) is found to be true.

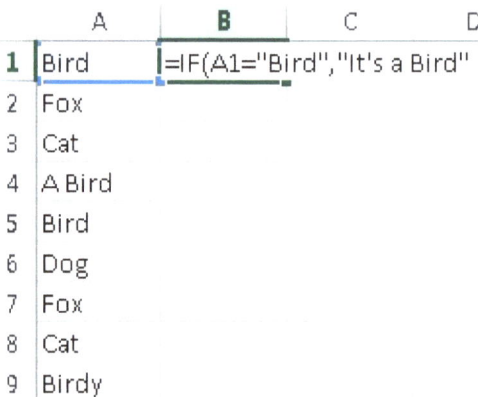

7. Type a comma to move to your next argument.

8. Input your final argument, in this example, "This is not a Bird". This argument is what is displayed if your logical test (from step 4) is found to be false.

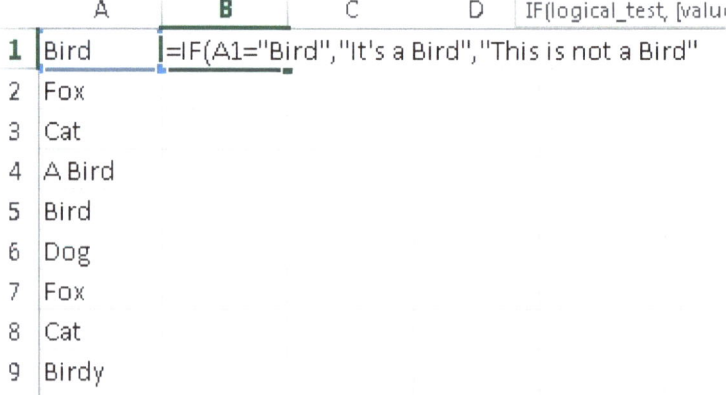

9. Complete the function with a closing parenthesis ")".

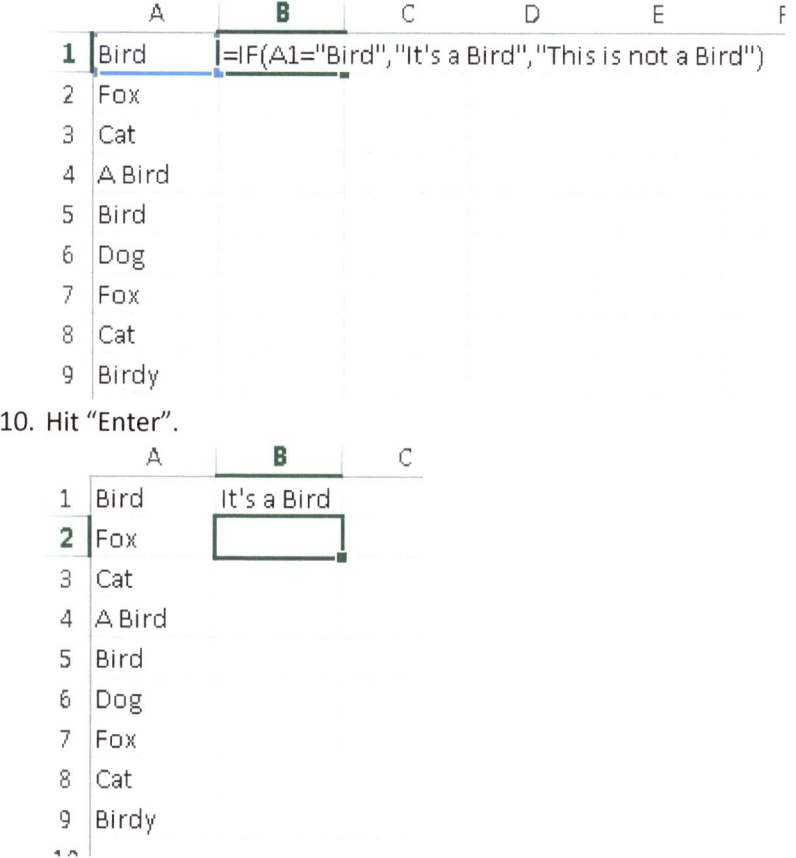

	A	B	C	D	E	F
1	Bird	=IF(A1="Bird","It's a Bird","This is not a Bird")				
2	Fox					
3	Cat					
4	A Bird					
5	Bird					
6	Dog					
7	Fox					
8	Cat					
9	Birdy					

10. Hit "Enter".

	A	B	C
1	Bird	It's a Bird	
2	Fox		
3	Cat		
4	A Bird		
5	Bird		
6	Dog		
7	Fox		
8	Cat		
9	Birdy		

11. Congratulations! You have used the If function! Remember that you can copy the formula and use it down an entire column or across an entire row. Below is an example of the same formula (using a different reference cell, "A1" through "A9") copied through cells "B1" to "B9" using the Fill Handle.

13

	A	B	C
1	Bird	It's a Bird	
2	Fox	This is not a Bird	
3	Cat	This is not a Bird	
4	A Bird	This is not a Bird	
5	Bird	It's a Bird	
6	Dog	This is not a Bird	
7	Fox	This is not a Bird	
8	Cat	This is not a Bird	
9	Birdy	This is not a Bird	

Additional types of logical tests:

Text:

A1 = "Bird" – Does the cell "A1" hold the word "Bird"?

B1 = "*Fox" – Does the cell "B1" hold or end with the word "Fox"?

H5 = "*Harp*" – Does the cell "H5" hold or contain the word "Harp"?

"trumpet*" = G5 – Does the cell "G5" hold or begin with the word "trumpet"?

Numeric:

A1 < 5 – Is the cell "A1" less than 5?

E3 <= 17 – is the cell "E3" less than or equal to 17?

Formulaic:

A3 + B3 = E3 + F3 – Does the sum of cells "A3" and "B3" equal the sum of cells "E3" and "F3"?

And many more… I encourage you to get creative and search for the proper syntax of your logical test if you do not have a good idea of what it might be.

IfError
Why is this function useful?

The IfError function will standardize different error messages in Microsoft Excel. No, it doesn't give you the ability to change the pop-up message box error messages. IfError, instead, will give you the ability to change the error messages that functions will leave behind. Instead of seeing "#N/A" or "#VALUE!" in a cell where the main function (or formula) wouldn't work you can write a custom message to say something more like "Value not found" or something as nonsensical as "I wish the plural of deer was deers".

It's hard to undersell this as well. Even beyond looking a bit more professional, there is definitely value in having a consistent message instead of a varied error message in your spreadsheet. I am thinking of using a CountIf function right now but consistency makes most things easier.

Description	Formula	Result
With IfError	=IFERROR(VLOOKUP(A1,C:C,1,FALSE),"Value Not Found")	Value Not Found
Without IfError	=VLOOKUP(A2,C:C,1,FALSE)	#N/A
With IfError	=IFERROR(4/0,"Divide Error")	Divide Error
Without IfError	=4/0	#DIV/0!

How difficult is this function to use?

This function is very easy to use.

How do I use this function?

1. Open Microsoft Excel and locate the data that you wish to use. Try to find functions that are already there. IfError is fantastic but, at least for me, is typically an afterthought.

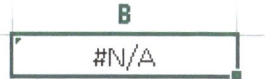

2. Activate the cell where you want to display the result of your logical test.

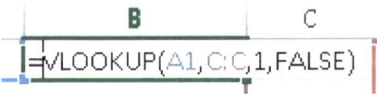

3. Type the IfError function after the equal sign but before the function that is already there, "IFERROR(".

4. Leave the function that was already there and add your custom message to the end of that function, in this example, ","This is my custom message"".

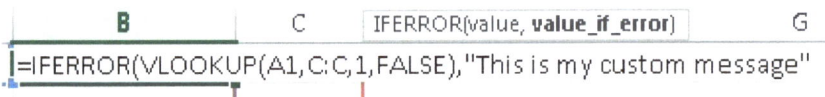

5. Complete the function with a closing parenthesis ")".

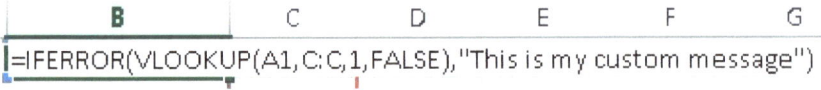

6. Hit "Enter".

7. Congratulations! You have used the IfError function! While this function won't ever be something that will make or break your sheet, it can really help to make your sheets look more professional.

IfNA

Why is this function useful?

The IfNA function will standardize only the "#N/A" error messages in Microsoft Excel. No, it doesn't give you the ability to change the pop-up message box error messages. IfNA, instead, will give you the ability to change the "#N/A" error messages that functions will leave behind. Instead of seeing "#N/A" in a cell where the main function (or formula) wouldn't work you can write a custom message to say something more like "Value not found" or whatever you feel is more relevant.

Even beyond looking a bit more professional, there is definitely value in having a consistent message instead of a varied error message in your spreadsheet. I am thinking of using a CountIf function right now but consistency makes most things easier.

Description	Formula	Result
With IfNA	=IFNA(VLOOKUP(A1,C:C,1,FALSE),"Value Not Found")	Value Not Found
Without IfNA	=VLOOKUP(A2,C:C,1,FALSE)	#N/A
With IfNA	=IFNA(4/0,"Divide Error")	#DIV/0!
Without IfNA	=4/0	#DIV/0!

How difficult is this function to use?

This function is very easy to use.

How do I use this function?

1. Open Microsoft Excel and locate the data that you wish to use. Try to find functions that are already there. If you have the foresight to add this to your formulas as you create them, fantastic!

    B

    #N/A

2. Activate the cell where you want to display the result of your logical test.

    B   C

    =VLOOKUP(A1,C:C,1,FALSE)

3. Type the IfNA function after the equal sign but before the function that is already there, "IFNA(".

    B   C   D

    =IFNA(VLOOKUP(A1,C:C,1,FALSE)
    IFNA(**value**, value_if_na)

4. Leave the function that was already there and add your custom message to the end of that function, in this example, ",""This is my custom message"".

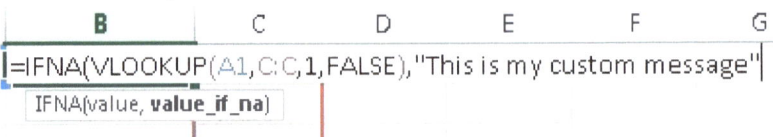

5. Complete the function with a closing parenthesis ")".

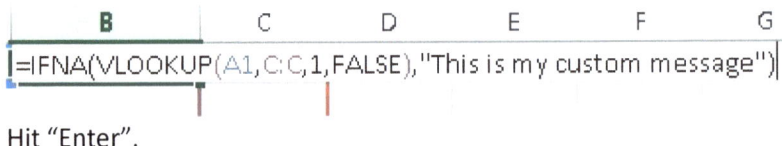

6. Hit "Enter".

7. Congratulations! You have used the IfNA function! While this function won't ever be something that will make or break your sheet, it can really help to make your sheets look more professional.

Not

Why is this function useful?

The Not function will analyze only logical tests and that single argument must be a full logical test. The Not function will only return "TRUE" or "FALSE" and will oppose the value found by the logical test. The key to the Not function is that it will give you the opposite of what you put into it.

This function is particularly nice to pair with the And or the Or functions. Nesting an And function inside of a Not function will allow you to analyze based on several criteria in the one argument. The If function takes the output of the Not function in the first argument just like the And function. Nesting an Or function inside of a Not function will allow you to analyze based on several criteria in the one argument as well. Just remember that the Not function switches the output to be "TRUE" or

18

"FALSE" as the opposite of whatever the logical evaluation is within the argument.

A few notable details about the Not function is how it handles different input. Take a look at the table below to see how certain input is handled.

Description	Formula	Result
True statement	=NOT(1+1=2)	FALSE
False statement	=NOT(1+1=3)	TRUE
Boolean input	=NOT(TRUE)	FALSE
Boolean input	=NOT(FALSE)	TRUE
Evaluation of a blank cell	=NOT(E6="")	FALSE
Evaluation of a blank cell	=NOT(E7=1)	TRUE
Numeric input (1)	=NOT(1)	FALSE
Numeric input (0)	=NOT(0)	TRUE
Numeric input (anything other than zero. Including negative numbers)	=NOT(143)	FALSE
Alpha input	=NOT(a)	#NAME?
NOT(AND(TRUE))	=NOT(AND(1+1=2,TRUE,E6=""))	FALSE
NOT(OR(TRUE))	=NOT(OR(1+1=3,1+1=2))	FALSE

How difficult is this function to use?

This function is very easy to use.

How do I use this function?

1. Open Microsoft Excel and locate the data that you wish to use.

2. Activate the cell where you want to display the result of your logical test.

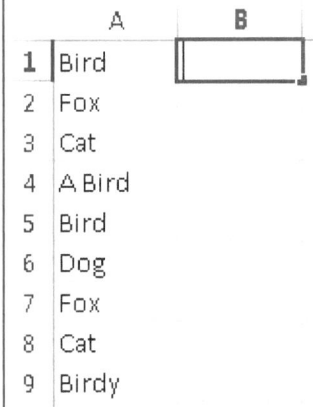

3. Type the Not function, "=NOT(".

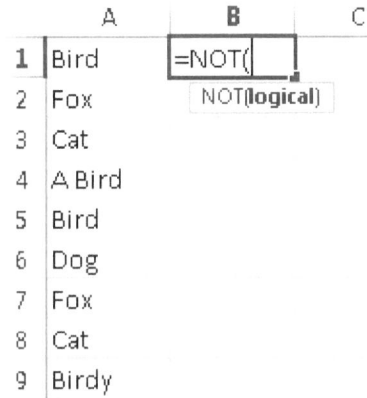

4. Input your argument, in this example, "A1="Bird"". This argument is the portion that you define the logical test mentioned in the description.

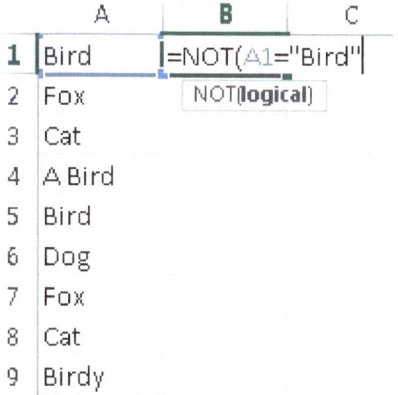

5. Complete the function with a closing parenthesis ")".

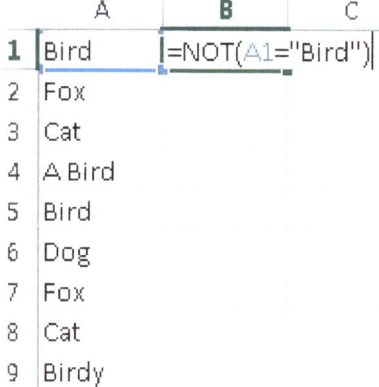

6. Hit "Enter".

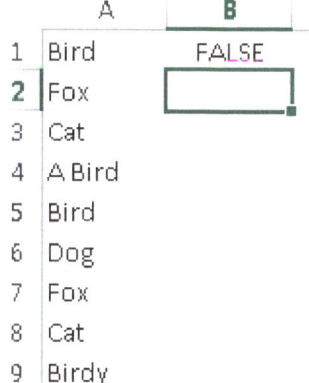

7. Congratulations! You have used the Not function! We entered a true statement into the Not function here and so it came back as "FALSE". Below is an example of what happens when you copy that formula down column B using the Fill Handle.

	A	B
1	Bird	FALSE
2	Fox	TRUE
3	Cat	TRUE
4	A Bird	TRUE
5	Bird	FALSE
6	Dog	TRUE
7	Fox	TRUE
8	Cat	TRUE
9	Birdy	TRUE

Or

Why is this function useful?

The Or function will analyze multiple logical tests. Each argument must be a full logical test. The Or function will only return "TRUE" or "FALSE" depending on the arguments. The key to the Or function is that only one argument must be true in order to return the "TRUE" value.

This function is particularly nice to pair with other functions like the If function. Nesting an Or function inside of an If function will allow you to analyze based on several criteria in the one argument. The If function takes the output of the Or function in the first argument.

A few notable details about the Or function is how it handles different input. Take a look at the table below to see how certain input is handled.

Description	Formula	Result
True statement	=OR(1+1=2)	TRUE
False statement	= OR (1+1=3)	FALSE
Boolean input	= OR (TRUE)	TRUE
Boolean input	= OR (FALSE)	FALSE
Evaluation of a blank	= OR (E6="")	TRUE

22

Description	Formula	Result
cell		
Evaluation of a blank cell	= OR (E7=1)	FALSE
Numeric input (1)	= OR (1)	TRUE
Numeric input (0)	= OR (0)	FALSE
Numeric input (anything other than zero. Including negative numbers)	= OR (143)	TRUE
Alpha input	= OR (a)	#NAME?
Multiple true statements	= OR (1+1=2,TRUE,E6="")	TRUE
True and false statements	= OR (1+1=3,1+1=2)	TRUE

How difficult is this function to use?

This function is very easy to use.

How do I use this function?

1. Open Microsoft Excel and locate the data that you wish to use.

2. Activate the cell where you want to display the result of your logical test.

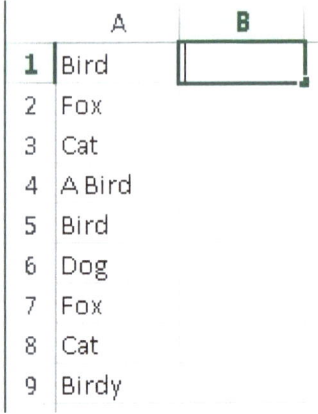

3. Type the Or function, "=OR(".

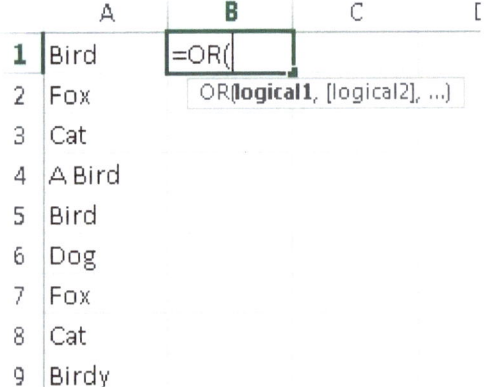

4. Input your first argument, in this example, "A1="Bird"". This argument is the portion that you define the logical test(s) mentioned in the description.

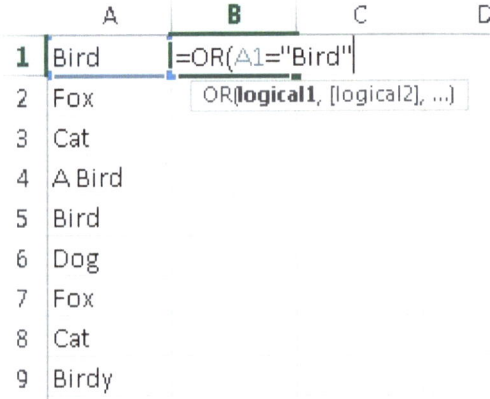

5. Type a comma to move to your next argument.

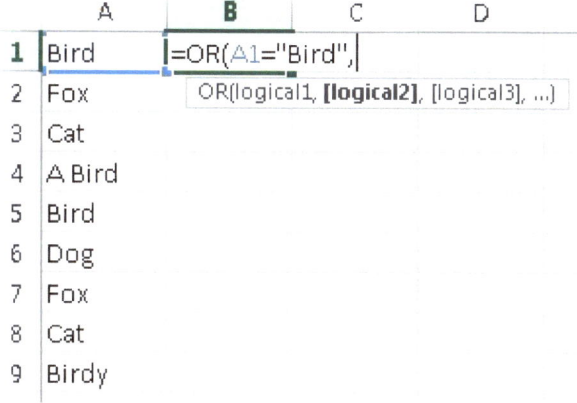

6. Input your next argument, in this example, "A1="Dog"". You can repeat steps five and six to accommodate your needs.

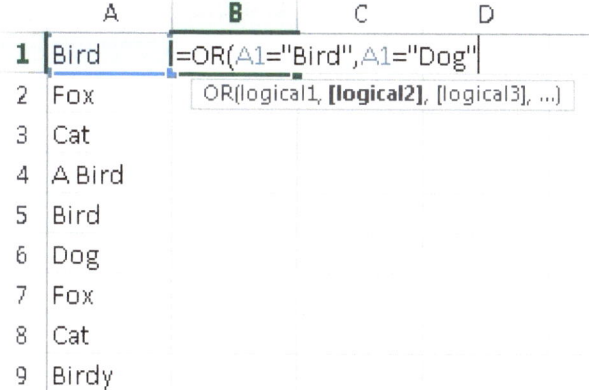

7. Complete the function with a closing parenthesis ")".

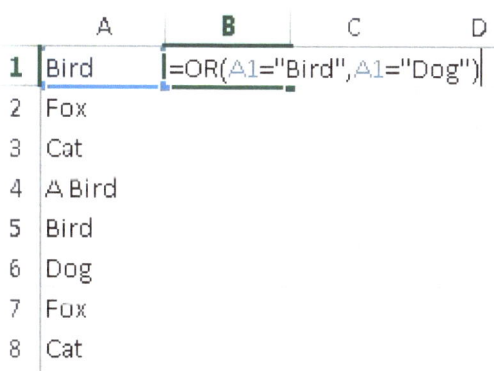

8. Hit "Enter".

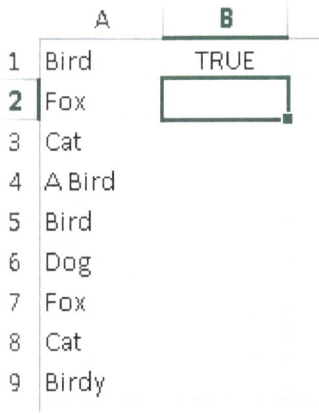

	A	B
1	Bird	TRUE
2	Fox	
3	Cat	
4	A Bird	
5	Bird	
6	Dog	
7	Fox	
8	Cat	
9	Birdy	

9. Congratulations! You have used the Or function. So now we have a true value if cell A1 is ever "Bird" or "Dog". This function is great to capture different triggers in your formulas. Below is an example of what happens when you copy that formula down column B using the Fill Handle.

	A	B
1	Bird	TRUE
2	Fox	FALSE
3	Cat	FALSE
4	A Bird	FALSE
5	Bird	TRUE
6	Dog	TRUE
7	Fox	FALSE
8	Cat	FALSE
9	Birdy	FALSE

True

Why is this function useful?

The True function in Microsoft Excel is particularly useful as a constant. The function itself has some fantastic properties. For one thing, the name is the purpose of the function. Secondly, and somewhat more useful to note, the True function will also work without adding parentheses. The True function already has no arguments so if you are using it within another function then simply typing "TRUE" will give you the same true constant that the True function will give you. The numeric

26

representation of the True function is anything other than the value of zero (0).

How difficult is this function to use?

This function is very easy to use.

How do I use this function?

1. Open Microsoft Excel and locate the data that you wish to use.

2. Activate the cell where you want to display the result of your logical test.

3. Type the True function, "=TRUE()".

4. Hit "Enter". There are no arguments in this function because it is actually a constant. You can even leave off the parentheses to complete this function.

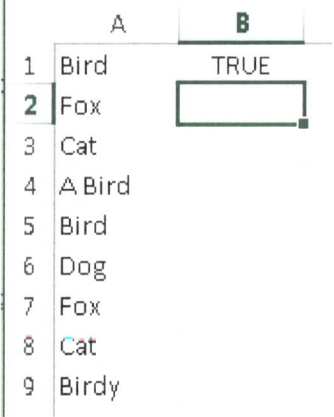

5. Congratulations, you have now successfully used the True function! Remember that you can use this inside any other function that takes a logical argument. The True function will return a constant True Boolean value.

XOR

Why is this function useful?

If you are already familiar with the Or function then you may want to consider it from that perspective. The only difference is that XOR (Exclusive Or) will only return true when ONE argument returns true. The XOR will return false if there are zero or more than one arguments returning a value of true.

The XOR function will analyze multiple logical tests. Each argument must be a full logical test. The XOR function will only return "TRUE" or "FALSE" depending on the arguments. The key to the XOR function is that only one argument must be true in order to return the "TRUE" value.

This function is particularly nice to pair with other functions like the If function. Nesting an XOR function inside of an If function will allow you to analyze based on several criteria in the one argument. The If function takes the output of the XOR function in the first argument.

How difficult is this function to use?

This function is very easy to use once you understand the difference between the OR and the XOR functions.

How do I use this function?

1. Open Microsoft Excel and locate the data that you wish to use.

	A	B
1	Bird	
2	Fox	
3	Cat	
4	A Bird	
5	Bird	
6	Dog	
7	Fox	
8	Cat	
9	Birdy	

2. Activate the cell where you want to display the result of your logical test.

3. Type the XOR function, "=XOR(".

4. Input your first argument, in this example, "A1="Bird"". This argument is the portion that you define the logical test(s) mentioned in the description.

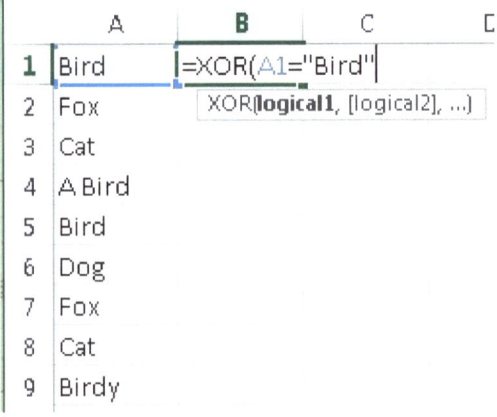

5. Type a comma to move to your next argument.

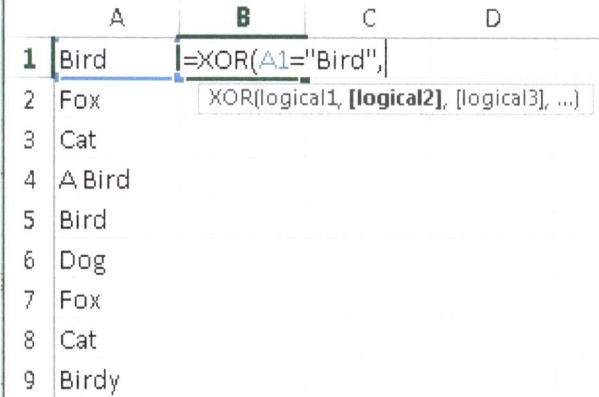

6. Input your next argument, in this example, "A2="Dog"". You can repeat steps five and six to accommodate your needs.

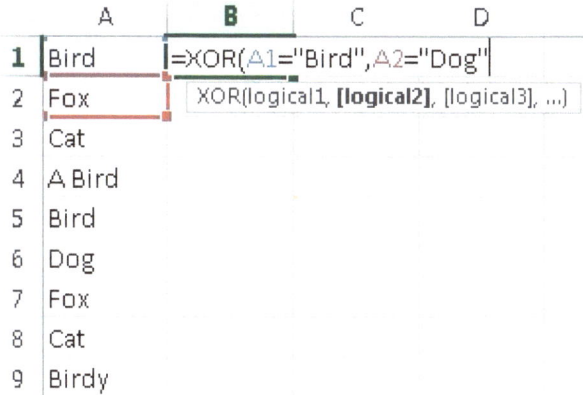

7. Complete the function with a closing parenthesis ")".

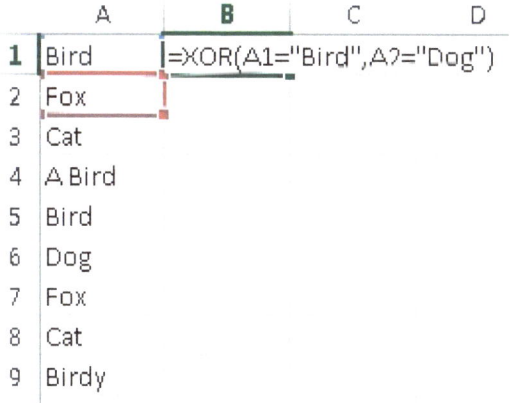

8. Hit "Enter".

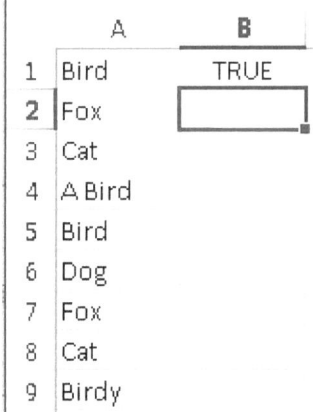

	A	B
1	Bird	TRUE
2	Fox	
3	Cat	
4	A Bird	
5	Bird	
6	Dog	
7	Fox	
8	Cat	
9	Birdy	

9. Congratulations, you have now successfully used the XOR function! Remember that the Exclusive OR function will only return true if only one of the logical tests will return to be true. If everything is false or if multiple true values are returned, then you will get a false response back from your XOR function.

www.ingramcontent.com/pod-product-compliance
Lightning Source LLC
Chambersburg PA
CBHW041612180526
45159CB00002BC/822